Apply for Disability On-Your-Own

Receive Your Social Security Disability Insurance Benefits in Just Four (4) Months!

I0134308

J.D. Davis

DP.O DavisPublishing.Org

Pasadena, CA

Apply for Disability On-Your-Own . . . Receive Your Social Security Disability Benefits in Just Four (4) Months!

By: J.D. Davis

Warning and Disclaimer: The information in this book is designed and offered with the understanding that it is to provide insight, understanding and guidance on the subject matter, and does not contain financial, legal or other professional advice. Whereas, every attempt has been made to provide accuracy of information in this book, errors and omissions can occur. The material in this book is provided "as is" without warranty of any kind. This book is not totally comprehensive. Therefore, readers requiring professional legal and financial services advice should consult a professional. The author and publisher assumes no liability for any damages that may occur from the use of this book, or alleged to have resulted in being linked with this book. There are no guarantees to receive Social Security Disability benefits and/or to receive said benefits within a specific timeframe.

This book is not authorized or endorsed by any mentioned company's service mark, trademark, product name or features and are assumed to be the property of its respective owner, and used only as a reference throughout the book. Also, this book is not authorized or endorsed by any implied organization, attorney, disability advocate, U.S. government, U.S. Social Security Administration and the U.S. Department of Social Services.

Published by: Jarita D. Davis
DavisPublishing.Org
Pasadena, CA 91105
First printing January 2015
ISBN: 978-0-9863876-0-9

To God be the Glory!

Dedication

FOR TONY L. DAVIS,
Beloved Husband, Friend, Partner, and Caregiver

And for the Memory of
My Mommy, Daddy, and Sissy
*For always encouraging me to pursue my dreams and passion, and to
"Always put God first."*

And to my loving brother and his beautiful wife, my sister-
in-law, John and Janet

TABLE OF CONTENTS

Apply for Disability On-Your-Own

Receive Your Social Security Disability Insurance Benefits in Just Four (4) Months!

LEARN how to handle your disability situation while applying for Social Security Disability Insurance (SSDI) benefits, and being approved the **"first time on-your-own"** without hiring an attorney, advocate…and **NO** appeals, **NO** courtrooms, **NO** judges, etc.

Be at peace and receive **ALL** of your SSDI benefits, while not being able to work due to your disability. You paid your FICA taxes for Social Security Disability Insurance, which is no different than paying for regular insurance – when in need – use it. SSDI is not a handout from the government, remember <u>you</u> paid into it!

www.applyfordisability-on-your-own.com

PROLOGUE

Ladies and Gentlemen, here it is. If you are looking for a book that will help you with understanding Social Security Disability Insurance and how to receive your benefits without going through attorneys or advocates and to receive your benefits **"on-your-own"** in just four (4) months, please read on.

You are about to join me on a passage through an experience of learning the process of becoming officially disabled and the need of emotional, spiritual, and financial support. Please know I am writing this book to help you – in sharing my story of successfully applying for Social Security Disability Insurance (SSDI), and, I was **APPROVED** the **"FIRST TIME APPLYING" on my own** with **NO assistance** from an attorney, advocate, referrals, and **NO** appeals, **NO** courtrooms, **NO** judges, etc., and **received my SSDI benefits within four (4) months**!

If you require a family member or friend to take care of your personal financial business, you may want to share this book with them to assist you in applying for your Social Security Disability Insurance benefits.

If you are mentally and/or physically dependent and have no one but yourself, then I recommend hiring an attorney and/or advocate to help you, and to read Part One of this book which may help you with learning more about yourself being disabled, and to help give you faith, hope and strength to keep moving forward in a positive manner during this time of your life.

IMPORTANT NOTE: **The Social Security Administration covers disability benefit payments through two separate programs. This book covers the "Social Security Disability Insurance" program only with proof of receiving timely benefits. This book does not include/cover the Social Security's Supplemental Security Income (SSI) disability program's process.**

So, let's get started with this journey. "Hello. My name is J.D. and I just had an appointment with my neurologist and learned that I would not be able to work my normal career path, and that I am now disabled." I've worked since being

15 years old, graduated from high school, went to college, acquired two degrees (i.e., BA, MS) and worked a total of 40 career consistent years. I was blessed to have two wonderful parents who wholeheartedly supported my vision and dreams, had a progressive and lucrative career, and married a wonderfully, hard-working and very caring and supportive entrepreneur. The two of us together have helped others, and had started to prepare for our retirement years. I have a beautiful step-daughter and adorable grand-daughter, who was born on my birthday. All was going well, until I received the news from my doctor -- that traveling, intense work, etc., and my fast paced career life would need to slow down tremendously due to a brain disorder. Ugh. Lord, help me.

Since 1979, I had always planned that if an incident of "disability" was ever to occur while working we would be prepared for it and therefore, always paid additional disability insurance through my employer. As many Americans caught in the middle of transition due to being disabled, etc., we were now placed in that situation with my career -- and with that said, "NO Disability benefits" were available through an employer or anyone else.

This has been a very huge eye opening experience of both learning and blessings which I have decided to share with others in this book. The first part of this book will help you in learning about yourself, hope, faith, and what is available if you ever find yourself being disabled. Also, it will help you learn how to adapt from the perspective of a person who became surprisingly disabled, and was successfully able to receive benefits from Social Security Disability by applying on their own with **no assistance from an attorney and/or advocate.** The second part of this book will disclose the "secret" in how to successfully apply and receive your "Notice of Award" in order to receive your SSDI benefits and start a new chapter of your life.

This book is written for you, if you are disabled, need financial support, and want to receive your Social Security Disability Insurance (SSDI) benefits in a short period of time versus become a part of the horror stories of waiting for a year or more; and to keep all of your hard earned benefits, versus having attorneys and/or advocates take a portion, when you CAN DO the application on your own, but was afraid to ask for assistance. This book will assist you in how to move through the application process, build confidence,

4

and receive your benefits in a timely manner. This book is not a technical book, it was written to be easily understood by applicants to apply for disability benefits, and receive their benefit award within four (4) months – on their own.

This book was not written for people to abuse the SSDI system to just use as a secondary welfare system which has recently been a subject in the media. This book is not to be used for fraud or waste of the SSDI system. It is a book to help people who are truly disabled, not capable of working and who need their Social Security Disability Insurance benefits in order to live life with purpose and to help them rest, be restored, increase faith, and heal emotionally and physically.

QUICK SUMMARY OF READING THIS BOOK:

Over the next few chapters of this book, you will discover how to receive Social Security Disability Insurance (SSDI) benefits by doing it yourself, AND receive your SSDI benefits in a few months as follows:

- Learning about yourself and making the "Disability" Decision

- Understanding Social Security Disability Insurance

- Can you "Do it Yourself" versus hire an attorney/advocate and keep ALL of your hard-earned money

- Learn the "Secret Factor(s)" in how to successfully apply on your own and receive benefits the first time submitted

- Receive Social Security Disability Benefits in just Four (4) Months by doing it on your own!

- The Beginning of a "New Life" Chapter – **FAITH & HOPE!**

"…as you are partakers of the sufferings, so also you will partake of the consolation."
–2 Corinthians 1:7 NKJV

PART ONE

MAKING THE "DISABILITY" DECISION

So – let's get started on "Making the 'Disability' Decision." First of all, what is the meaning of "disability?" Or, should I ask, "What does this 'disability' terminology mean, since that is what I am now being classified, at this moment?"

I might sound a little perturbed about this subject, because it is all new to me and is not what I expected to deal with in life. But, I am realistic that "things happen to all people," and I am very thankful to God for my faith and hope of this being a temporary season, coupled with a new life of learning, purpose, and sphere of influence that will hopefully help many people in our nation who are going through the same situation or condition.

The American Heritage Dictionary of the English Language, 4th Edition, defines: "disability – 1a. The condition of being disabled; incapacity. b. The period of such a condition: *never received a penny during her disability*. 2. A disadvantage or deficiency, especially a physical or mental impairment that interferes with or prevents normal achievement in a particular area. 3. Something that hinders or incapacitates. 4. A legal incapacity or disqualification."

After reading the definition of "disability" from the dictionary, it brought me to tears. That is not me! I am fine. I am not that person. Well, the definition brings light in learning who I have become during this period of life of being classified as "disabled."

Okay – STOP! Yes, this is real, and I just had a quick "pity party" for myself. It is normal to have a "quick" pity party, and it is wise to release your pity and move on with faith and hope for your future.

Now, with that said, it is time to move on to claim and make an affirmation that the "self-pity parties" are OVER. Dear Reader, you will not experience another pity-party in this book, because it is now time to take control, take action, and learn about yourself, so that you can prepare to move into your new stage of life by accepting and embracing your disability season, coupled with finding means to help rest, restore, renew, heal and survive physically, emotionally and financially. To that end and moving forward, let's get to work!

LEARNING ABOUT YOURSELF

Let me help you, and share how I first reflected and focused on learning about myself. **STEP 1**: Recommend at this moment -- you take time to reflect -- by remembering and visualizing your first job and/or a section of your past. Are you ready? Following is my story. Here we go!

My work career started in 1973. The current year is now 2014. I will always remember my first job of approving credit for a national retail department store. When customers wanted to purchase an expensive or large ticket item, the sales person would call the main Credit Department, and ask for credit approval. I would be on the other end of the telephone, and would search for the name of the customer from large customer credit volume books, and review their credit payment history and credit data for the past six months to eventually make a decision to either grant or reject credit for this customer.

At that time, no one had any awareness that a 15 year old girl in Pittsburgh, PA was approving credit for families and was standing up at a counter in booty socks because there were no chairs available for us "credit authorizers" to sit during the work hours of approving/rejecting credit. *(I guess that's why teenagers were hired versus adults)* It's amazing how you reflect back on your life not being aware of the impact you may have had on people's lives – such as approving credit for a family to purchase a refrigerator, washer/dryer, television, etc.

But, I was happy and glad to know of my purpose, and that I would get paid for it. When I did receive my paycheck, I noticed taxes were taken out and one "big tax" item taken out was FICA. What was that? Who cares at 15 years old, I was getting paid to save and spend a little. I'll figure this FICA thing out later in life, which is why I'm writing this book to help people understand it sooner than later. It took me a long time to understand its purpose, and it has been an unexpected blessing to me, my family, and to people I have helped along the way to learn about Social Security, especially SSDI – Social Security Disability Insurance.

With that said, this book was written for you. In order to help you learn about SSDI, I feel it is important to share with you my dreams as a child to my adult work life as it helped prepare me to give you this information. As mentioned, Part I of this book covers preparedness thoughts for mental and emotional changes in your life; and Part II is focused on specific steps and avenues in how to apply and receive your Disability Benefits within four (4) months.

STEP 2: At this time, think of your personal life and a story after you graduated from high school and/or started working consistently every day. To help you with your "thought" I'll continue with my personal story:

As mentioned, I started working at the age of 15 years old after school hours. Graduated from high school at the age of 17, and went directly into college and acquired my Bachelor degree. I was very fortunate to be recruited by a Fortune 50 corporation on campus and started working in a management capacity with 40 direct reports in Chicago. Wow! It was noted, I was one of the highest paid graduates from our graduating class. What an accomplishment! My parents and I were happy and proud of this achievement, and it helped me become driven with determination to become successful in the business world, and to financially plan for my future.

I was a workaholic, a master in multi-tasking, can-do, always going the "extra mile;" promoted every year at my first corporate management job, and maintained a progressive career path to my last corporate assignment as an operations vice president leading offices in California and Illinois for a large global financial services corporation.

In 2006, I made a decision to resign from the corporate world to help my family in dealing with an aging parent and family illnesses. I was able to help our family make the transition, took a break and then went to work in the non-profit arena in Development or Advancement *(professional fund-raiser)* to raise funds for children/students in schools, children in camps with life threatening diseases, churches, music, children from foster homes, and non-profit organizations -- and was very successful in linking people together to raise millions of dollars for these various causes and loved it! My days were busy in both the corporate and non-profit worlds and I believed in 24 x 7 days to work the causes, but now I'm disabled. Like many people who make the transition from work to being on disability – I had to face it and accept it for its temporary time period.

So, you may ask, "What led you to write this 'disability' book?" To start, my natural self and passion is to help people of all colors and all walks of life. I personally know people from various socio-economic backgrounds, for example: individuals who are regular working people, upper class, middle class, underserved, homeless, millionaires and billionaires; and religions i.e., Christians, Jewish, Muslim, new age, and non-religious individuals, etc. and believe me everyone has issues. People are all different in beliefs, life experiences and action, but everyone lives through "good" days and "rough" days. *(I do not believe in "bad" days, therefore, you will read in the book, the replacement of "bad" with rough.")* How people handle their life is an individual decision, and should be unconditionally respected.

Personally, I learned from my first job in 1973 to today, that my "purpose and work life" are very important to me. My parents would always remind me to put God first in my life;

they injected the importance of strong work ethics, family and to play later. With that said, the priority of growing into adulthood – was and is to stay focused as a believer and follower in Jesus Christ, have a successful career and purpose, family commitment, etc. and that is what I believe. And, to answer the aforementioned question of what led me to write this book there were **five** main reasons, as follows:

REASON #1: All my life, I've dreamed of writing books that would help people. For example, during my corporate career, I had the wonderful opportunity to serve as an operational vice president for eight years, for a fabulous major publishing house in Boston, and learned about the publishing world, hoping that one day I would be seated at the after-work dinner table as an author versus working in publishing management. So let's say writing this book has been a long time dream and vision that is now coming to fruition. After I was awarded my SSDI, I felt a deep calling to write this particular book to help individuals who are finding or have found themselves in my same predicament of learning about disability and how it affects a person's life.

REASON #2: My wonderful husband Tony, felt I should use my gift of writing that I used for 26 years at multi-billion dollar corporations -- to write this specific book of encouragement to help people learn about disability, SSDI, and for them to keep their hard earned money, and that I should share my testimony regarding the importance of having faith and hope in unplanned and difficult times.

REASON #3: While pondering about writing this book, a light bulb lit up, and I realized the "importance" of purpose and work, receiving an annual W-2 or 1099, and for those 40 years of paying FICA taxes from every paycheck, it helped me to enhance my retirement future with Social Security benefits, in addition to retirement fund (i.e., 401K, pension plans, IRA, etc.) programs. I would sometimes grumble about the large FICA amount and taxes taken out of my check, but did not give it a second thought because it was taxes for the government. Taxes have to be paid, and it is all good.

REASON #4: In work life, it is helpful to share what you have learned that was not confidential as it relates to individuals and job-related circumstances. As mentioned, I served 26 years in corporate America and acquired senior management and leadership positions and responsibilities for multi-billion dollar companies. It was an awesome opportunity of learning and growth to serve at a senior management level in the conglomerate corporate world. My main areas of expertise were operational management, design, development, and implementation of operational areas, project leadership, and customer/client services. I found having that type of corporate background as being very helpful and resourceful when completing the SSDI application. This was due to my ability and gift to process operational environments, work flows, service transactions and reversing it from a company aspect to a customer viewpoint. Having that gift is the "secret" purpose of Part Two of this book, in how you can complete the SSDI application by yourself versus hiring an attorney or advocate.

As mentioned, Part Two will show you from a SSDI applicant perspective, how to move through the application process expeditiously, and receive your Notice of Award within four (4) months of applying for SSDI. My neurologist was very surprised and impressed when she asked me about the status of my SSDI application. She called me at home one late afternoon to find out what attorney I used so she could let her patients know who to contact for SSDI assistance. I told her I did it on my own, and she recommended that I should write a book to help patients because of their immediate needs for financial support, and their fear from the many SSDI horror stories regarding delays in applying for SSDI. This is an excellent segue into my last reason for writing this book.

REASON #5: The last reason is two-fold: (1) for me to share my knowledge, gifts, and passion to help others and; (2) to exercise my brain. Since we're getting personal, I had two (2) major brain surgeries within a two month timeframe. *(i.e., a story of its own)* So, if you wonder why the book came out over a year later from receiving my Notice of Award, I had to write this book during my "up days" of focus, which were initially far and few in between at times. It is a journey that I'm continuing to learn from and very thankful to God. I hope this book will assist others, as it has helped me exercise my brain and thought process.

In closing this section, remember earlier I mentioned "FICA?" This is part of the money you have paid as a tax to the government on every paycheck you ever received listed on your annual W-2 form. You are not a welfare case, because you paid into your SSDI. Again -- remember you paid into your Social Security Disability Insurance, and do not be embarrassed to say you're on disability. It's all good. For your benefit, please remember this paragraph as it will help you understand, as we segue into our next sub-chapter: **REFLECTION.**

Reflection

The American Heritage Dictionary of the English Language, 4th Edition, defines: "**reflection** – ...3a. Mental concentration; careful consideration. b. A thought or an opinion resulting from such consideration. 4. An indirect expression of censure or discredit: *a reflection on his integrity.* 5. A manifestation or result: *Her achievements are a reflection of her courage...*"

Let's do a quick review of this chapter thus far, "Learning about Yourself," and how this will help you "reflect" for future success of applying for SSDI, and moving forward with your new life. First and foremost, put "yourself" into my shoes and remember when your doctor told you or implied the possibility that you were disabled and strongly recommended you could not work for a long period of time. Right now – let's take 10 to 15 minutes and "reflect" on that moment and meditate on how you felt when you were told. While reflecting, think of the following questions. 1.) Did you feel that moment was surreal? 2.) Did you believe it or disbelieve the diagnosis? 3.) Did you think about your family, and how were you to provide to help keep the household afloat? 4.) Did you think what others would say? 5.) Did you feel inadequate and helpless? 6.) Did you even care to think about being disabled?

While writing this book I will continue to interject personal situations that occurred and it will assist in keeping the book to date and what this situation is – reality. For example, yesterday and today I spoke with 2 different senior ladies: one a stranger and the other a friend. The subject of "disability" came up during our conversations. I have not been publicly open with all family and friends to let them know I'm on Social Security Disability Insurance (SSDI), but it came up just today and yesterday with these two ladies. In both cases, both ladies were not totally aware of the SSDI process and what SSDI is all about.

One lady thought it was similar to unemployment benefits. Both individuals mentioned they never had to use disability and the stranger implied it was beneath her, such as being on welfare or she is already prepared for health financial issues with long-term care insurance. Big difference! Will long-term care insurance pay for buying a book, medicine, food, dress or pantsuit? I am reflecting from these two conversations that some people have a stigma against SSDI. They see it as being for the "poor" or those "unprepared" for retirement. Please note both of these ladies did not mean any harm, are highly educated, single and with no dependents. So, my answer to the aforementioned, Question #4: "Did you think what others would say?" should have come to light.

Many people do not totally understand the SSDI purpose and process. Both ladies were in their mid-60's drawing Social Security retirement benefits, and that was appropriate by them – but it felt questionable to receive Social Security Disability Insurance prior to retirement age. **My recommendation:** do not be ashamed to apply and receive SSDI benefits, *(remember the last subchapter's last paragraph and me requesting you to remember it)* but, if someone does ask your reason for being on SSDI, be prepared to state your case of why you applied and remember to discuss the comparison of Social Security "retirement" benefits and Social Security "disability." From experience, that should stop the questions, and you can smile inside. Please remember -- you paid FICA taxes for both benefits. If your doctor states you cannot work for a long period of time – use your SSDI benefits. It is no different than paying for insurance – when in need – use it.

You may have noticed from my writings, discussing SSDI with others is sensitive to me, such as, people speaking about something they have no clue, no experience, or knowledge about – but still want to help and give their opinion. I personally need to rise above it and proceed without getting upset. God bless them, and for your own comfort please be prepared to hear opinions and move on with the positives of learning through your season, as I am doing with my season. Personally, I learned my "sensitivity limitations" lesson, and will probably not discuss the subject with others in the future, unless the question comes up in a conversation, or we're talking about this book.

Now that I have risen above the compromised negatives –
let's reflect on the **positives**. First of all, we should all be
very thankful for the Social Security Disability Insurance
(SSDI) program. The next chapter will focus on, "What is
Social Security Disability Insurance?" – but now as we reflect
– let's take a moment of silence to appreciate the program
and to mentally and emotionally get prepared to start going
through the application process in plans to receive the end
results – your Notice of Award! In preparation for a mental
flow process of successfully applying through your reflection
. . . let's next focus on what is occurring at this present
moment. Let's continue to move on with the process and
segue to **"Present Day Thoughts."**

Present Day Thoughts

Today was a rough day. I had plans to write all day, but felt
unable to barely get out of bed. These types of days come
and go. I am very thankful to God for these days, because
the day reminds me of how far I've come by having faith and
hope, and then I reflect on not being able to work 9-5 or not
having energy to travel, meet and greet, and not being crazy
busy with life and enthusiasm. Ugh. I promised earlier in the

book, pity parties would be short and limited. Hmmm – just had one. Pity party is over. J.D., move on!

Okay -- I'm feeling better today! Ready to write:

My present day *"disability"* thoughts vary. Some days I feel that I can go back and be the old active J.D. and work 24 x 7. Other days, I face the reality of my condition which is treatable, but not curable at this time. I believe and feel positive that one day there will be a cure, and I hope and pray to be part of that wonderful day and to be healed. In the meantime, I work hard to be a positive Christian woman, and hope this season will be a blessing to many people in helping them "quickly" acquire their SSDI benefits, and for them to have some peace of mind financially during their disability period.

At this time, I recommend you take this moment – right now – and put this book down, get a pen and paper, and write your "present day thoughts" *(i.e., write down how you're feeling today and at this moment)* and date it. I had to do this. I keep it in a safe place and recommend you do the same. It's always good to review your writings for encouragement and inner peace. My dearest Cousin Hazel (to whom I call

"Mom" now) is a retired English/Literature professor and poetic author. She recommended that I should "think and write" something every day as a journal, after having my first brain surgery and to jot down how I was feeling. She was not aware, she was encouraging me to write this book, and that a sub-chapter would be created because of her advice and recommendation. It's always good to reflect on how you're feeling, so when you acquire your SSDI Notice of Award you will be fulfilled to know that your positive thoughts, meditation time, writing down your thoughts, coupled with faith and hope were not in vain. Relax and enjoy this quiet time of being alone, and to write, reflect, and prepare for the next sub-chapter, "Faith and Hope."

As you're coming out of your quiet meditation period, let me share with you another personal conversation I had with my late Uncle Warren *(who just passed away today)*. On a separate note, one positive interaction that may happen if you're seriously ill is the love received from family members, friends and their support. It is always a blessing to hear from family members and friends who may live far away for encouragement, especially when you're physically suffering. My late uncle was very inspirational to me as a child, and has been supportive of both my husband and me during this season. He helped me think about making the decision to apply for SSDI. He let me know to not be ashamed to request SSDI, because, as we mentioned earlier, I paid into Social Security and people who paid are entitled when needing disability insurance support in order to help them move forward, and to help keep a roof over their heads and pay health insurance.

When I first shared my thoughts of applying for SSDI with my late uncle, I was a little embarrassed. I'm one of many family members that worked hard in the corporate world in upper management, always helped out family members emotionally and financially, and was known to have my act together. My husband and I together had a significant six-figure income, lived on a country club-guard gated community in Southern California, etc., etc. At various times, we had relatives actually tell us they were jealous of our success, but they also admired our nature of quietly giving and helping others, and my stamina and resilience since I had multiple surgeries while still being employed before the two (2) recent brain surgeries. Now the situation had reversed. Fortunately, many of our relatives continue to have good health, still work with solid careers, or they're enjoying retirement and can function, and unfortunately at this time in my life, I cannot work because of my illness. I had no company disability benefit insurance; and prior to this, I always had coverage to prepare for the unexpected. Now – no coverage and we were living in a high mortgage/rent area. But, all is well and I thank God for my faith, my wonderful husband, family, and friends who helped us to move forward and focus on taking next steps for a brighter day.

Faith and Hope

It's been 22 days of no writing. My days have been rough, memory issues, head pains, and foggy. I thought it was only two (2) days of not writing, but, I date my writing days and counted 22 days. Reality has set in. I must continue and what better chapter to start and help in getting us through this season than, "Faith and Hope."

During this time, reality really sets in and you have to release all of your doubts, fears, and anxiety. Every day is good, and some days are rough. *(NOTE: 'days' are not bad)* While waiting for your SSDI approval, you can take on a very anxious state of mind. But taking one day at a time is highly recommended. Do not think of tomorrow, just get through today and you will be just fine. It's good to plan and have short and long term goals, but, when your health is being compromised it is mentally safer to relax and take one day at a time and put all long-term goals to the side until your health is stable.

With that said, during the application period the main focus is to concentrate on your doctor's guidance and your SSDI application process. We'll talk more about this in detail in Part Two.

This sub-chapter is short, but extremely important – have "Faith and Hope." If you believe, all will be well for you emotionally, spiritually, and physically. Your body will relax and be open to complete your SSDI application process with less anxiety and a "can-do" manner of approaching your goal and the end-result – your Social Security Disability Notice of Award!

Next Steps

Your next steps are to *"prepare for success"* in order to complete the SSDI application process, and to receive your SSDI Notice of Award in just four (4) months. Preparation will entail becoming comfortable with your subject by learning more about the purpose of Social Security, Social Security Disability, alternative options, answering preparedness questions and studying Part Two of this book, as it relates to achieving your mission by receiving your Social Security Disability benefits in a timely manner.

WHAT IS SOCIAL SECURITY DISABILITY INSURANCE?

In order to proceed successfully with the Social Security Disability Insurance (SSDI) application process, it is important to actually understand, "What is SSDI?"

The Social Security Administration (SSA) website, which is: "www.socialsecurity.gov" section on history greatly explains the origin of Social Security, Social Security Disability, Medicare, and I recommend you visit the website to learn of the origin and purpose of Social Security and SSDI. Please note: it is not necessary at this time to review it, but for general knowledge it is a nice read and gives an appropriate awareness to the subject.

For example, per the Social Security Bulletin, Volume 60, 1997, Number 2, states: *"Disability benefits under Title II of the Social Security Act became part of the law in 1956, and*

Medicare came into being in 1965. We might assume, therefore, that the first cash disability payments made by the Social Security Administration (SSA) occurred sometime around 1956, and the first medical benefit claims would have been processed sometime around 1965." With that said, there are numerous Reports & Studies researched and published on the www.socialsecurity.gov/history website and the data is very interesting as it relates to how long the program(s) have been in existence and original purpose(s).

But, for a quick reference and real understanding of SSDI and "Disability Benefits," the best answer to the question of, "What is SSDI?" can be found on the www.socialsecurity.gov website in the Social Security Administration (SSA) Publication No. 05-10029, ICN 456000, page 4, as follows: *"Disability is something most people do not like to think about. But the chances that you will become disabled probably are greater than you realize. Studies show that a 20-year-old worker has a 3-in-10 chance of becoming disabled before reaching full retirement age...We pay disability benefits through two programs: the Social Security disability insurance program and the Supplemental Security Income (SSI) program."*

NOTE: this book and the SSA Publication No. 05-10029 covers **ONLY** the Social Security disability insurance program. If you need information on the Supplemental Security Income (SSI) program, please visit the website (www.socialsecurity.gov) and review the publications for the SSI program.

The aforementioned quote from the SSA Publication says it all. It is so true, many of us do not expect our bodies to become disabled, but, sometimes they do – and we should make all attempts to be prepared if it does by chance occur in our lifetime. Again, this is a quick reference to assist you in understanding the Social Security Disability Insurance program. The next quote from the SSA Publication also on page 4, briefly describes the program exceptionally well, as follows: *"Social Security pays benefits to people who cannot work because they have a medical condition that is expected to last at least one year or result in death. Federal law requires this very strict definition of disability. While some programs give money to people with partial disability or short-term disability. Social Security does not."*

With that said, the above quote is a solid segue to our next sub-chapter, "Is it True?"

Is It True?

Throughout Part One of the book, it will always mention the importance of learning and knowing yourself. Please believe me, this "disability" journey is up and down, and it is imperative you attempt to stay focused, be at peace, and know thyself. To that end, in order to proceed successfully with an expeditious SSDI application process, it is extremely necessary to "deeply" understand and accept your current situation, and internally answer the following question about your disability, and that is, "Is it true?" If your doctor or medical practitioner has advised you that working full-time/part-time is not for your best interest, or that you should not work due to your medical condition; or your family has given an intervention that you listen to your physician and not work – the answer to, "Is it true?" is "Yes. It is true."

If you have worked for many years, it is so very hard to accept the fact that you are being told ". . . you are disabled." It's hard. But, now it is time to face it – and take a quiet

31

moment to meditate, pray, and ponder the moment, and then verbally say, "Yes. It is true." and move on with the realization, and then proceed with reviewing all of your disability benefit options.

Alternate Disability Options

If you are an employed individual and have "disability insurance" as part of your health and employment benefits – awesome! Now is the time to advise your employer of your situation and apply for your employer's disability benefits, if available. Some employers offer disability insurance as a benefit. The employer's disability benefit insurance is different from the government's Family and Medical Leave Act (FMLA) program. The disability insurance benefits from employers' are usually between 60-80% of your salary or pay. **NOTE:** Every company is different, therefore, please verify your company's disability program for your position with your Human Resources department. You could have the option to accept that amount and conserve other disability monies regarding the difference. If you are unemployed or employed, you may have an option to apply for temporary State disability, if your state offers it and this could help supplement your income and/or the difference of your wages. Additionally, many insurance companies have disability programs that are offered, and you may want to research those avenues. But, since you are reading this book, you are probably already in a "potential disabled" manner, and obtaining disability benefits from an insurance company should be a research option for later, not now.

If your disability is assumed to be longer than a year, now is the time to apply for Social Security Disability Insurance (SSDI) which is available for the rest of your life, if your disability remains. Please note, there are periodic medical reviews based on your specific claim. The medical reviews are performed by hired SSDI medical professionals over a period of years, to re-evaluate your disability case.

To summarize the alternate disability options to research, are as follows:

1.) Employer short-term disability program
2.) Employer long-term disability program
3.) State disability program
4.) Insurance companies
5.) Social Security Disability Insurance (SSDI)

Remember to always check with your Financial/Tax professional regarding your specific situation. Now, let's move onto making the "major" decision of who should administer your SSDI application process, **"you or an attorney/advocate?"**

The Process Decision – "Them or Me?"

We have discussed learning about yourself, reflection, present day thoughts, faith and hope, and alternate disability options. The last "Alternate Disability Option" we briefly covered in the last subchapter was, "Social Security Disability Insurance (SSDI)." After learning about my inability to work a full time career, and not having available a long-term state disability coverage, individual disability insurance coverage and/or employer disability coverage, I had to research the Social Security Disability Insurance (SSDI) program.

I found out that after working for 40 years, the FICA tax that was taken out from my paychecks since I was 15 years old, could help support me during this time frame in my life. Wow! SSDI is available for individuals who have worked, paid FICA tax and need financial support to help with everyday needs. We had planned for retirement, but, with me being disabled and my husband being my caregiver since we did not live near family, we had to expeditiously focus on making the decision to apply, in order to help maintain our standard of living.

We heard interesting and horror stories of how long it takes to receive SSDI – if approved! All we were hearing is that it may take years to receive your SSDI Notice of Award, but, you would receive a "back payment" lump sum for your wait. Social Security Disability Insurance benefits are paid for the sixth full month after the date your disability started, and monthly benefits are based on an individual's average lifetime salary or wages.

We were hearing it could take 2-5 years and to use an attorney or advocate. We heard using an attorney/advocate would help relieve stress, in not having to worry about filling out loads of paperwork. It was also mentioned to let the attorney/advocate just perform the application processing, because they would be able to push the paperwork through the system while you rest, but, the timing of receiving your benefits could be a long waiting process. Sounds good to have it done by a professional and to not worry about paperwork, but, the waiting period and not having control during this critical time was not a "feel good," but more of a "stressor" to the overall situation.

What a decision to make. After working in a corporate "operational" environment from manager to vice president levels, I felt there had to be a way to bridge it all together and for the system to work in my favor. If I could work through the application process "on my own" with success, I made a promise to publicly share my story to assist others. I strongly believed it could be done, and set a goal to receive my disability benefits within four (4) months.

Happily – the strategic process was successful and within four (4) months, I received my Social Security Disability Notice of Award. I'm humbled and honored to share this information with all of you, and wishing you the best in your decision making. Everyone's situation is different, and some of you may need to hire an attorney/advocate – and it is wonderful they are available to help those in need of their services. If you need an attorney/advocate to help you, I recommend you go on the Internet to find a disability attorney/advocate listing or ask around for word-of-mouth referrals.

To that end, I found it very ironic while writing this book, and surprising, that the television series 60 Minutes aired a segment on "Disability, USA" on October 6, 2013. Wow! What an affirmation for writing this book and sharing another viewpoint of Social Security Disability Insurance. It was an excellent segment that educated its viewers on the U.S. Disability Fund, and how SSDI is used by American people who are unable to work due to illness or injury.

The CBS 60 Minutes segment initially aired on October 6, 2013, and rebroadcasted on June 29, 2014 mentioned the Federal Disability Program provides service to approximately 12 million people and has a significant budget of over $130+ billion. To compare with other government departmental budgets, it was acknowledged this budget (in 2012) was larger than a combined budget of the Justice Department, Labor Department and the Department of Homeland Security.

The segment also covers the Federal Disability Insurance Program's positives by explaining it is available to assist people financially who have been disabled, and are unable to work. It also covered some disheartening facts such as it being perceived as a secret type of welfare system, coupled with various fraudulent activities, etc.

To put it mildly, the segment also opened up many questions and concerns about the Federal Disability Insurance Program *(Social Security Disability Insurance)* program's representation of claimants by attorneys and/or advocates. For example, it was mentioned in the early 1970's, there were less than 20% of claimants represented by attorneys/advocates, but now, it is perceived as the way to go – get an attorney, kick back, and let them do the work. ***My two-cents:*** *remember attorneys have to be compensated, and the longer the process the better for them, since they will receive payment from the government and also many will receive a percentage of your disability insurance back-pay, etc.* Moving on – it was also mentioned the claimant representation of 20 percent in the 1970's has now increased to over **80%** of representation by attorneys/advocates. What a difference time makes…

This book was written to help potential disability claimants complete the Social Security Disability application process **"on their own"** and to **"keep all of their hard-earned money."** Part Two of this book will clearly explain the

38

potentiality of "how to receive your SSDI benefits within four (4) months."

As the question in the title of this sub-chapter states, "The Process Decision – "Them or Me?" is where we are in – how **"you"** will plan to apply for Social Security Disability Insurance. For example, should you hire an attorney and/or advocate; or should you have a family member or caregiver help you with applying; or can **you just do it on your own**? As mentioned in the Prologue, there are many avenues you can take to apply, but, if you can:

1. Read with understanding,

2. Use a computer comfortably,

3. Feel comfortable and confident to speak on your own behalf to an SSA representative and,

4. Believe you can take control and apply on your own to reap your benefits, then the answer to the sub-chapter title question is "Me!"

To build confidence in taking your next step with this journey, say to yourself and speak loudly, "I can do this. I will do it. And, I will complete the SSDI application process and receive my disability award benefits within four (4) months on my own!" **YOU** can do it! I did it, and received my disability award benefits within four (4) months – and so can **YOU**! Let's proceed immediately, and move forward to the **"take action"** section – **Part Two!**

PART TWO

IMPORTANT NOTE – MUST READ

The information in Part Two is based on a true event, and the process of an ever-changing Internet. Please note some of the information may be slightly outdated with some enhancements due to Social Security Disability Internet updates, but, the process of the upcoming **"Secret Factors"** are still very viable in receiving your Social Security Disability Insurance benefits within a timely manner. **NOTE:** there are no guarantees to receive your Social Security Disability Insurance benefits within a four (4) month timeframe (every individual situation is different), but, this system works to expedite and process business transactions in general. **Godspeed and much success to you!**

WHAT'S THE SECRET?

There is no algorithmic method to successfully apply for Social Security Disability Insurance (SSDI) and receive your benefits within a four (4) month period. But, first of all, I strongly recommend you use the Internet to apply. The Internet process helps record your entries, keeps you and SSDI simultaneously on track, and is an excellent tool to expedite the application process because it is in real time and data does not get lost in the paper shuffle or on someone's desk. It is well documented and the Internet application will become your best friend while applying for SSDI.

Secondly, there is an essential systematic process called, "System Work Flow," and a human factor methodology of learning the art of handling people interactions that we'll call, "conduced Customer Intimacy (cCI)," coupled with having patience, stamina, and perseverance.

The overall secret comes in two **"secret factors of focus:"**
Secret Factor #1 (SF#1): System Work Flow
Secret Factor #2 (SF#2): People Interaction/conduced Customer Intimacy (cCI)

You may ask, "What's so secretive about system work flow and people?" Good question, and there is a good answer for it. But before we continue with the answer, please read the following. ***<u>IMPORTANT NOTE</u>***: if you are interested to learn the **"reasoning and explanation"** of how to receive Social Security Disability Insurance benefits within four (4) months, please **continue to read this entire chapter**. If you want to go straight into learning **"how to" start your SSDI application process without delay,** then proceed directly to the next chapter, **"What to Do Now?"**

Moving on – the answer to the aforementioned question of, "What's so secretive about System Work Flow and People?" is as follows: these two **"secret factors of focus"** greatly influence the end result of the applicant being approved to receive a timely SSDI Notice of Award. Therefore, it is essential the two "secret factors of focus" overlap and touch the end result being "SSDI Benefits."

For example, let's review the three circles below:

System
Work Flow

Social Security
Disability
Insurance (SSDI)

People
Interaction/cCI*

The circle in the middle represents SSDI Benefits. It is the end-result of our mission in quickly receiving benefits. The two circles on each side have to overlap and/or touch the

SSDI circle. With the two circles touching the middle circle, it brings cohesiveness to the entire SSDI application process.

The circle to the left represents the "System Work Flow" **secret factor of focus** regarding the SSDI application process. The System Work Flow is what compounds and creates the ability to receive your SSDI benefits. What generates its success in order to expedite SSDI benefits approval results, is the managing of "System Work Flow" touch-points.

For example: a System Work Flow "touch-point" could be your first "personal" entry into the SSDI Internet application program, and what occurs afterwards. A "touch-point" can be described when you are entering data into the Internet application – then you are "touching" the system to initiate action for your application. The following chapter will explain the application process and the importance of System Work Flow.

The circle to the right of the SSDI Benefit is called the "People Interaction/cCI*" **secret factor of focus**. As mentioned earlier, "cCI*" stands for "conduced Customer

Intimacy" and is defined as, "leading a specific result to build a proactive customer-type relationship with a constituent." It covers the "people" focus of the secret.

For example, when an applicant receives a notice or confirmation of receipt, etc. from an SSDI office, the contact person's name and contact information are usually typed in and made available to the applicant. Many times, we'll look at the listed name and file it, or even throw out the document.

The document/contact information is considered a "touch-point" within the "cCI" or "People" circle. This person is essential to your application being processed and "their name and who they are" will become "golden" to your SSDI benefits being expeditiously received.

Therefore, it is extremely imperative that you, 1) keep the document close at hand and do not discard it; and 2) build a positive and real cCI relationship with every SSDI contact name that is given to you via mail, email, fax, telephone, etc. For example, if you're talking on the telephone with an SSA representative, engage in a one minute conversation and ask them how they are doing, etc. Showing "sincere" care and concern to the SSA representative could be helpful to them that day, and possibly yourself.

To summarize and review: the middle circle is **SSDI,** which is the end result to receive benefits in a timely manner. The circle to the left of the SSDI circle covers the **"Secret" System Work Flow** and is essential to ensure data is communicated to all parties; and the circle to the right is the **"Secret" People factor** of building a relationship with SSDI staff in keeping current with the data flow, etc.

In order to understand the "secret" it is necessary to comprehend the **"System Work Flow"** process and **"People Interaction and/or cCI-conduced Customer Intimacy"** factors of focus. Once you understand those terms and the importance of managing them you will immediately "get it" and will know the "secret" of how to process your SSDI application, and to expect receiving benefits within four (4) months. Please do not be alarmed by the terminology or these written words. Believe me, it will be easy to understand.

So, let's start with the "System Work Flow." This area is essential in actual application processing and acquiring your end result of SSDI benefits. First of all, there are two separate areas of System Work Flow – you (the applicant) and the Social Security Administration (SSA). We'll start with the System Work Flow that is about you, and we'll call it "System Work Flow-you."

For example, it is very important that **you** focus on **your mission,** and follow-up with SSDI personnel on <u>every</u> occasion available. When you receive documents via any media of communication or telephone calls, always closely read the information and/or take the calls. For the information/data that is distributed to you from SSDI personnel, it is extremely important and imperative that you closely take time to review it, and promptly respond back as noted in the requested information. If "System Work Flow-you" is not on top of the situation and current, your SSDI application processing will be delayed and you can forget about receiving your Notice of Award in a timely manner.

Therefore – **always heed** to **all** communications and **promptly respond**. For example, medical examinations may be required and you should immediately respond, establish

47

your appointments, and be prepared with all required and requested documents for that medical examination appointment. If you wait and let the documents sit in your mailbox or on the kitchen table, and then you decide a week later to make an appointment, etc. a delay in your SSDI Notice of Award will be evident.

Secondly, the System Work Flow of the Social Security Administration (SSA) in processing your SSDI application is essential. Your life as it relates to receive SSDI benefits is in their hands. The "System Work Flow-SSA" is just as important as "System Work Flow-you." As an example in layman terms – we will discuss overall large corporations and government operations.

At this time, many large corporations and government operations have numerous divisions, departments, teams, etc. that compounds the organization. The corporate areas mentioned usually have a specific mission with goals. These goals are eventually reviewed, discussed and built into strategic action plans where leadership or management establish ways to meet those goals. For example, a goal could be to process 5,000 applications in a specific amount of time.

It is usually management's responsibility to work with their staff to establish an action plan to achieve those goals. When this occurs, there could be many mission goals that may or may not overlap with other areas. This is usually the case, and these individual operating areas tend to work in a "silo environment."

So what is a "silo environment?" Since the late 1980's, the term, "silo" has been used to explain how departments/people work independently of each other in boundaries, focusing on their own departmental goals and purpose.

Simply defined, every operating area has their own mission, but may not communicate their mission or goals (including customer needs) to other work areas and vice versa. With that said, the collaboration of work flow does not touch, except for transference of data for that specific area to work for their own mission.

In "silo environment" layman's terms, every department has their own mission, but does not know what other departments are focused upon – only their own. This type of environment may paralyze progress and the movement of an application may be stifled. There is nothing you personally can do to change this business model, but, you can help take control of your application by interacting with your designated contacts within those individual departments/areas.

In closing, when a silo "wall" is weakened or removed from your SSDI application, it "triggers" the departments/areas staff to feel ownership and you will notice the SSDI staff will want to help with your application process, due to a "real" relationship being built between you and the SSDI staff.

IMPORTANT NOTE: *at the time of this writing many progressive companies are utilizing new and highly effective technology and organizational development initiatives to remove the "silo environment" and are successful with the development and execution of Customer Relationship Management (CRM) programs. As a result, it improves productivity and efficiency levels for the organization, where all required customer contact employees and staff can view a customer's interaction within the company. This aforementioned customer relationship management (CRM) process helps build a closer customer intimate relationship* *between the customer and the company/organization. For example, if you call a utility company, and a customer service representative answers the telephone, they may already know who you are from caller ID. They may request you to answer account verification questions, and from your answers they can access and view your account in the computer CRM system, such as the last time you called, a last visit from a utility technician, billing questions, etc. When representatives access data from "customer interfacing" departments within the company, they can usually handle your transaction within a "one-call" resolution versus transferring your call to various departments, etc. that could take hours or even days to resolve.*

To that end, this smoothly segues into our next secret area of "conduced Customer Intimacy (cCI)" or "People" factor. In order to move the application process along, it is very important that human interaction is used in a "positive" manner. In life it is important to treat people the way you want to be treated, and that same rule applies here and is necessary to help expedite your SSDI application process.

The key to creating a cCI connection is to build a "real" relationship with each designated SSDI department contact person who is introduced via email, mail, fax, etc. It is key to always follow-up on each transaction and date/time stamp all communications. How to build a true relationship is to be real and truthful. Always be positive and appreciative of every SSDI contact person. It is extremely important that your relationship building with everyone involved is "true and real." Do not put on an act. People will feel an act, and it's not for this purpose.

Go deep within yourself and make these moments of building relationships real with humility. Positive effects will come from your authenticity. Also, it is important to always project a professional, yet kind manner, when interacting with SSDI staff. For example, when on the telephone, put a smile on your face and always thank them for helping you. A smile does actually penetrate through the telephone. It really does. It can be felt. Try it. This action will help remind the SSDI staff representative that behind every application is a "human being" needing their help and assistance.

Overall "Secret" Keys to Success:

- Help remove or breakdown the silo "wall" environment for your application by being professional and positive when interacting with your designated SSDI contacts. This will help you in gathering next step information on what to expect, and how to potentially proceed with your SSDI application.

- Always respond back immediately to communications from the SSA in establishing all areas of processing, such as, document requests, establishing medical examinations, etc. Do not procrastinate at any level of communications.

- It is important to follow-up, document, and let your SSDI contacts know your needs and build a relationship from the beginning to the end result of receiving your SSDI benefits.

- Build a "real" relationship with each designated SSDI department contact person.

- Project a positive image, that is appreciative, professional, confident and yet kind when interacting from all communication vehicles.

ANOTHER IMPORTANT NOTE! This book was specifically designed and created to give you "tips" and "recommendations" on how to move through the Social Security Disability Insurance process in an expeditious way, and when/how to act in order to receive your Disability benefits in a faster manner. With that said, whenever a tip or recommendation is implied, there will be an outlined message to acknowledge which "Secret Factor" (SF#1: System Work Flow or SF#2: People Interaction or both) is being activated and/or used during your application process.

WHAT TO DO NOW?

There are many stories about how long the SSDI application process takes, who gets paid and when, such as attorneys and advocates being involved, and how to apply. Since I opted to "do it on my own," it was time for me to apply and start the process. Following is how I started my SSDI application, and I'm honored to share my personal experience and give helpful tips as follows:

In order to assist me to remember the date I initially applied on the Internet was very helpful, and that date was acknowledged by the SSA. The date my mother passed away on November 19, was the date I applied and began the application process. At first I was uncomfortable to apply on that date, but, I was perusing the SSDI website two days prior (Nov. 17) and decided to go ahead and apply on November 19th. My reflection of the day I lost my mother was very sad and yet peaceful, because she would no longer suffer on this earth. Five years prior to that date, she had a massive stroke and my Dad cared for her every day. She had lost her left leg, being amputated due to diabetes, paralyzed on left side of her body and for those five years after her stroke, my husband and I commuted from Chicago to Pittsburgh one weekend per month to help Dad take care of Mom, and to check up on him.

It was fulfilling to help, and yet it opened my eyes to watch this very confident, vibrant, prayer warrior, caring, and can-do woman change in front of my eyes to being paralyzed in a wheelchair with difficulty speaking. She was a blessing to many people, and always had an outreach to people less fortunate than us. She was a beautiful and strong lady. To that end, my Dad was the epitome of a wonderful husband, who always said he was committed in taking his marriage vows seriously and to heart, and that he would take care of my Mom and he did. Words cannot express my love and appreciation for my own wonderful husband, Tony, who traveled with me to help my parents during that timeframe, and we have been happily married since 1989, best friends forever and he has been my caregiver. . . I love you, Tony.

Memories of my mother helped me with the process to apply for my SSDI benefits on her day of no more suffering on this earth. Also, applying on that date helped me when communicating with SSDI personnel.

SF#1: System Work Flow For example, when an SSDI representative would look up my records and request the date I started my Internet application, I knew immediately it was November 19th with a smile of gratitude. **Recommendation:** initially apply via the Internet on a special memorable date, that will give you a reflection of good memories, hope and confidence. I did, and four months later received my SSDI Notice of Award. I also recommend using children's birthdates, anniversary dates, etc. something positive and memorable that will help give you confidence and a "can-do" manner of broaching the SSDI application process.

Start Your Application Process

As mentioned in our last chapter's first paragraph, "What's The Secret?" it is highly recommended from experience, to use the Internet to apply for your Social Security Disability Insurance (SSDI) benefits. Per the SSA, located in their Adult Disability Starter Kit, is the following first statement, "We encourage you to begin the application process online." It is highly recommended that you read the Social Security Disability Starter Kit information, which is located on their website at www.socialsecurity.gov and search for Adult Disability Starter Kit.

The Starter Kit has a checklist that gives you information to prepare for your application processing in general – either via online *(preferred method)*, telephone interview or in person at local Social Security office.

The Starter Kit also helps in your preparedness to: 1.) ensure you meet the requirements to apply online and; 2.) collect the data required to complete the Disability application process for SSDI. As stated, the SSDI Internet online application program – records and saves your entries, and is an excellent real time tool. So, let's not delay and start your application process now!

Here we go:

Step 1:

- Go online to:

  www.socialsecurity.gov/applyfordisability

- And, that's it!

The "Apply Online for Disability" webpage is rich with information, and should make you feel comfortable with the start of your application process. Since I applied, the SSDI office has been continuously enhancing their website and program information, therefore, I highly recommend you review this webpage closely, and also click to "review and print-out" the pdf's listed under Publications.

As of September 2014, the .pdf Publications noted on the webpage are: 1) Apply Online for Disability Benefits and 2) Disability Benefits. (See reference pages) In summary the first publication gives you the: why to apply online, security of system, how to apply, data collection requirements, etc. Additionally, the "Apply Online for Disability Benefits" publication explains the two separate areas of the SSDI application process as follows:

1.) Disability Benefit Application
2.) Adult Disability Report

Please note, the above are two separate processes that are two separate entries. For example, the Disability Benefit Application requests information such as, verification of the following: social security number, U.S. citizenship, employment, bank information, etc. The Adult Disability Report is more directed towards your illness and requests verification of who you are, type of illness, medical and employment history.

The second .pdf publication "Disability Benefits," covers many aspects of the SSDI program, such as disability benefits, when to apply, family benefits, Medicare, etc. and is more informational summarizing the overall Social Security Disability Insurance program.

Again, the Social Security Administration has done an excellent job in keeping the SSDI Internet application data updated and has made exceptional enhancements since I applied back in 2012. Kudos to the Social Security Administration and the SSDI office!

If your comfort level is mediocre in using the Internet, there are two other methods to use in applying for SSDI and those are:

1.) Call Social Security at 1.800.772.1213 to set-up an appointment to meet with your local Social Security Office to personally file a disability claim, or

2.) Call the aforementioned telephone number and request to make a telephone appointment, and have a representative take your disability claim over the telephone.

SF#2: People Interaction/cCI As mentioned, the Internet is the preferred method to expedite your claim and can be more easily recorded and tracked. But, if you need to file via telephone or local office appointment, it is highly recommended to closely review the aforementioned Adult Disability Starter Kit's section: **"Checklist – Adult Disability Interview"** which goes into detail by giving a checklist for the disability benefits eligibility interview via telephone or in the local office.

Always remember to be "Prepared, Professional and Polite" to whomever you speak and meet with – and those 3 P's will be on your side to help with your SSDI process being moved closer and closer to receiving your SSDI Notice of Award.

DISABILITY BENEFIT APPLICATION

As previously mentioned, there are two (2) separate areas of the SSDI benefit application: Disability Benefit Application and Adult Disability Report. The first section is the **Disability Benefit Application** or (Application for Benefits), and we'll discuss this area first.

When applying online, the day you register and set-up your online account is the date the SSA will use as your "official registration date" for the application. As mentioned, my date was November 19, 2012. Wow! It was official! You are given six (6) months to complete the application (with your e-signature) or "you may lose Social Security benefits."

Per the SSA, "If this date falls on the weekend or is a Federal holiday, we (they) must receive the signed application by the following business day." So, to keep this real, as mentioned – I initially applied on 11/19/2012 and officially completed my first section of the "application" on 11/29/2012. (**PLEASE NOTE:** this completion was for the "<u>first</u>" section only, and was **not** for the entire application being completed.) How did this 10 day process happen? Here's the answer: SSA gives an **Application Number** that is active for the entire application process, from the first initial date of Internet entry into your application to receiving your decision being made on your SSDI application.

ANOTHER NOTE: the "Application Number" they give you is a **keeper**. **<u>DO NOT</u>** discard or misplace this number, and definitely **<u>DO NOT</u>** share it with anyone. This provides total access into your SSDI application. This **Application Number** stays with you during the entire application process, even during the "waiting period," and it is the access in checking your SSDI Application Status – by entering this Application Number along with your Social Security Number.

To answer the above "10 day question" – here is the answer: during that ten (10) day timeframe, I was able to update my application when able, and always had to use my Application Number…in order to regain access into my SSDI application. It was great! All you have to do is:

1.) Type in the following website:
   http://www.socialsecurity.gov/disabilityonline

2.) Click "Return to a Saved Application"

3.) Next, type in your Social Security Number and "Application Number" then, hit enter.

The system will take you directly back to your last entry on the application. That's it!

VERY IMPORTANT NOTE: SSA advises the following, **"If you lose or forget your Application Number, you will have to begin this application over again and you will lose all the information you already entered."** To that end, always remember the Application Number is a keeper and to – **keep it close**. Also, if for some reason you are not able to return back to your Internet application, and still want to apply for SSDI via another method, just call the Social Security telephone number at 1.800.772.1213, and they will have representatives available to assist you.

Now back to personal sharing: please know the evening of November 29, 2012 was a "happy and fulfilling" night for me! Yay! I officially received an online confirmation from the SSA that my "first" section of the claim application was completed and received on November 29, 2012 at

9:33:21PM. Amazing! Also, the online confirmation gave information for next steps which was to complete my online Adult Disability Report (SSA-3368) and medical release form, "Authorization to Disclose Information to the Social Security Administration (SSA-827). Let's first briefly cover the medical release form.

The SSA developed an online medical Authorization Form for applicants to review and e-sign. The online medical release form is automatically filled-in with your personal information and it only requires a "click" to accept. In summary, it takes all of one minute to review and e-sign your medical release Authorization Form, and then it is done.

SF#1: System Work Flow Now, there are options to print and mail the Authorization Form to your local Social Security office, but, that does compromise speed in receiving your SSDI benefit claim processed expeditiously. Friendly reminder – time is of the essence, and taking time to either mail or visit the local office could potentially compromise a couple of days in processing and receiving your SSDI benefits. It is **strongly recommended** to process the medical release Authorization Form **online and use your e-**

signature. Remember to always "print and file" this form and all documents during your application process.

SSDI RECEIPT LETTER AND CONFIRMATIONS

After you receive an online confirmation of your application being completed, a hard copy letter of acknowledgement and additional information will arrive to your mailing address from the Social Security Administration's Disability Insurance (SSDI).

SF#1: System Work Flow This letter will again confirm receipt of your Disability Benefit Application, and explain if additional information is needed in order to complete your total application, as it relates to directing you to complete the Disability Report online. Also, the letter will give your local Social Security Office address, telephone number and your Representative's name with their telephone number and extension.

SF#1: System Work Flow and SF#2: People Interaction/cCI Now is your time to take **immediate action!** Once you receive the hard copy letter with a request for additional proof of income and your local contact person information, it is now time to contact that person, in order to help expedite the request for additional data. (i.e., proof of income, etc.)

[RULE #1: Contact your local Social Security Administration contact representative immediately, once you receive their information to start building your "one-on-one" relationship.] If your SSA representative is not available and your call goes to voicemail, leave a message with your name, telephone number, and claim number. Also, leave a brief message and explain the purpose of your call. Your telephone call purpose is to introduce yourself, and to request a brief discussion of how to send your proof of income to that person or office in an expeditious and approved mode of communication.

Since we're keeping this real, I did have to call numerous times and left voicemail messages. After leaving the voicemail messages, I was happy to receive a call-back, and that call was golden. Yay! My SSA representative was apologetic of the call-back delay and also empathetic to my calls. That person wanted to help expedite my claim, and versus having me mail in the documents requested, they gave me the "FAX" number to send the proof of income via fax.

The SSA representative also wanted to stay connected, and that started the building of an "on-going" relationship.

SF#1: System Work Flow and SF#2: People Interaction/cCI

[RULE #2: Always find out what FAX number can be used to expedite your application processing.] My SSA representative gave me their fax number and this significantly reduced turnaround time of overall "snail mail" (mailing via U.S. Postal Service and SSA in-house mail processing). No matter on what occasion – when information is requested and for it to be mailed in – ask the SSA representative this following question, "How can we expedite the process, and can I use your fax number to send the documents?" Every time (100%) an incident occurred and I would ask this question to "fax versus mail" – every time – the SSA representative would say "yes" and they gave me their fax number to send what was requested.

SF#1: System Work Flow and SF#2: People Interaction/cCI

Always ask for your SSA representative's **fax number**. The fax request will move the Secret Factor #1: System Work Flow and build a Secret Factor #2: People

Interaction relationship quickly. For example, one time I faxed over 20 pages in one incident, and the turnaround time was phenomenal for the request. Think about it. From the time it takes you to compile the information and place it in an envelope – mail it – have it received and placed through in-house mail to be stamped – sent from the mail room to the SSA representative and then placed in their "inbox" could be days.

Again – ask for the FAX number and fax it. Within 5 minutes the information is sent and received. Also, always keep and print-out your fax transmittal receipt page to ensure confirmation from an electronic viewpoint. And then, call the SSA representative back to verify with them, that you sent the fax and request their confirmation that – they are in receipt of the fax.

Okay. Stay with me. We have covered: confirmation of first section of application being completed, hard copy received of confirmation and additional documents needed, "secrets and rules," medical release form, and fax versus mail, which are **extremely IMPORTANT** to manage in order to expedite your application.

In closing of this segment, the first section of your application, **"Disability Benefit Application"** is completed. We will now segue to the second section of the process and that is the, **"Adult Disability Report (ADR)."**

ADULT DISABILITY REPORT

As aforementioned – let's get back on track with the application process, and move into the **ADR**. Now you should go and sign back into your Internet online application, and start on the **Adult Disability Report (ADR)**. As mentioned, this report is separate and even has its **"own" re-entry number** to sign-on/off and return later in order to complete the report. Please note you **cannot use your earlier Application Number to re-enter into the Adult Disability Report.**

If you need to take a break and return back to the Adult Disability Report and continue on . . . you must keep the "Reentry Number" for access back into the Adult Disability Report system for updates.

The Adult Disability Report requests and covers more details of explaining your illness, such as list of doctors, medications taken, prescribing doctors, medical tests, employment, education, and insurance/worker's compensation claims. Therefore, it may take time to complete the report in order to ensure accuracy of your claim. It is highly recommended to be rested and complete the report in a couple of Internet sessions. The Reentry Number will be given to you, along with a new website to access in order to complete the Adult Disability Report (ADR).

[RULE #3: Take your time to complete your entire application, especially the Adult Disability Report section. It is imperative you ensure accuracy and triple check your data.] Ensuring accuracy will avoid potential issues, which in turn could alleviate rejection of your SSDI claim. I strongly recommend you use your option to re-enter the Adult Disability Report by using your Social Security Number and Reentry Number. The website will explain how to sign-off, but, always remember to click the "Sign Off (finish later)" option. SSDI will save your data, and when you are fresh and ready, you can proceed back to the report:

1.) Go to the website:

www.socialsecurity.gov/adultdisabilityreport

2.) Click the "Go back to the Report |Already started" option
3.) Type in your Social Security Number and your Reentry Number

As a tip – just like the Application Number keep the Reentry Number close at hand and **DO NOT** share it with anyone. On a great note – with your Reentry Number there are no limitations on the number of times you can access the Adult Disability Report system. Awesome!

Per the SSA, **"IF YOU LOSE YOUR REENTRY NUMBER BEFORE YOU SUBMIT THE REPORT, YOU WILL NOT BE ABLE TO GO BACK TO THIS REPORT AND FINISH."** You would have to begin a brand new Adult Disability Report and would receive a new Reentry Number. Per the SSA, no one can help you regain access without your Reentry Number and, "all of the information you previously entered will be lost." In summary, **protect** your Adult Disability Report: **Reentry Number**. Ensure you do all you can to **not lose or discard** your Reentry Number.

As promised, we are keeping this book real and succinct for your reading and learning purposes. As a friendly review, from 11/29/2012 to 12/10/2012 I worked on the Adult Disability Report (ADR) updating it numerous times and triple checking it for accuracy. After much thought and getting to the point of your mission, I will not cover the entire Adult Disability Report (ADR) but, feel compelled to bring one very special section of it to your attention when completing the report **SF#2: People Interaction/cCI**.

One area on the ADR that is extremely imperative to **complete in detail** with passionate and clear thoughts is the last section, called **"Remarks."** This is your way to express what you have been going through, your needs, and asking for approval of your benefit claim. It is your expression to the reader to understand your disability and how it has impacted your life in the past, present, and future. To leave this section blank, or to just doodle a note or two is not acceptable as being a **Secret Factor** in expediting your SSDI application.

Once again -- **REPEAT**, **SF#2: People Interaction/cCI** is activated in the **"Remarks"** section. This section is the time to tell **your story**, express **your passion**, request **your need** for a benefit claim approval, and last but not least, **build a relationship** with the staff person reading/reviewing your records. Do not be ashamed to state your case and tell your story to the reader. I hope my duplication of explaining the "Remarks" section – has expressed its sincere importance, and that it should be written in an explanatory, passionate manner – in order to explain and **ask for approval** and to also **expedite** your claim benefits, so that you can **focus on healing** and **regain a new, solid purpose in your life** towards **moving on**.

While working on the Adult Disability Report (ADR) during that timeframe, I had no interaction with SSA staff only the Internet application and staying focused towards getting the ADR completed and submitted. The day is now December 10, 2012 at 7:16:29 p.m. Eastern time, and my ADR was just completed via online. Yay! I received a "Receipt for Your Records" confirmed notification that my "Online Adult Disability Report and electronically signed and dated Medical Release Form" were received. Another Yay! It is done!

CONNECTION WITH LOCAL SOCIAL SECURITY OFFICE

From the point of the online "Receipt for Your Records" notification confirming your entire Claim Application which covers: 1.) Disability Benefit Application *(previously confirmed)*, 2.) Adult Disability Report, and 3.) Medical Release Form electronically signed and dated – the application process is then moved towards being administered by your local Social Security Office, and next steps are advised.

Per the SSA, "It takes about 120 days to make a disability decision. Every case is different. We may take more or less time on your case." Wow. The notification also addressed more information may be needed, such as the potential of more medical evidence being required – where the SSA may request the claimant to visit one of their doctors at no charge.

Additionally, the "Receipt of Your Records" gives next steps, contact information for the local Social Security Office, and a copy of the completed Adult Disability Report. This receipt is very informative and helpful in reviewing the submittal and is a "keeper."

[RULE #4: Keep all receipts and confirmation notices received by SSA close at hand, and do not share with anyone unless that person is assisting with your application, and needs to process your personal identification data and disability information.]

Moving on in real person application time – the date and time is now December 27, 2012 at 3:19 p.m. Pacific time and a form letter from the local SSA office was generated to send an "Application Summary for Disability Insurance Benefits Confirmation Number" letter, titled "Checking the Status of Your Claim," along with instructions on how to access your claim status. The document indicates a small waiting time period (approximately 5 days) before being able to check claim status, and it gives the SSA webpage for claim access.

SF#1: System Work Flow

The letter also noted a confirmation number for the claim and to remember to guard this number carefully. As noted, this is the "Confirmation Number" that is key to your entire application. The SSA advises to not store this number with other personal information and to not give it to anyone. Most important: it is also noted, "Social Security employees will NEVER ask for your Confirmation Number." And, not to scare you – but the following is noted in the letter, "…disability claims take longer to process than other types of Social Security claims because we need to obtain sufficient medical evidence to show that you are disabled." As mentioned – please do not get scared, so now is the time for you to acquire patience, meditation, perseverance, and reflect on how great it is to have this opportunity and look forward to the future. Approximately a month will pass by, and it will be a quiet month of patience and probably an excellent time to read a good book. Remember, the process is occurring and no news is good news for this time period!

Medical Examinations and other Documentation

So…to continue sharing my journey in real time – from December 27, 2012 to the first of February 2013 was a quiet time period, which was to be expected. My doctors and the hospital staff were very accommodating and quick to respond to the SSA medical record requests. Many thanks to my doctors, their staff and hospital staff. But, we know patience is a virtue and it was now February. So, when Monday February 4th came around there was some anxiety on my part to find out next steps. I calmed down and reminded myself that Mondays are usually not good days to resolve issues or ask questions in a business customer service environment.

Therefore, I waited until Tuesday, February 5, 2013 at 1:51 p.m. *(after lunch time)* and activated **SF1 and SF2**, and then called the local Social Security Office. It was Tuesday, and they happily advised me of next steps for my application, and that it was now in another department and division. The Department of Social Services was the new department, and the "Division of Disability Determinations (DDS)" was under that department. The SSA representative offered to transfer my call to the DDS analyst scheduler to find out the status of my claim. | SF#1: System Work Flow |

HELPFUL TIP: before a business call is ever "offered to be transferred," always remember to request that actual telephone "number" before the call is transferred – in the event the call is not transferred with success. This new Division was a critical point in the application process, and the need to expedite with "no call transfer issues" was of the utmost importance and urgency. Therefore, I **"immediately"** requested the Division's telephone number just in case the call transfer did not work. Fortunately, the call transfer was successful. But, if it was not, I would have had to start back and call the local Social Security office for information, and start the new division contact process over again.

When the DDS analyst scheduler answered the call, I put on my "professional, polite face" and spoke with the analyst scheduler and immediately began building a relationship. At that time, it was discussed there was unfortunately, **no one** scheduled on my claim. "Ugh." After we discussed the situation and more relationship building, by the end of the call, a "Disability Evaluation Analyst (DEA)" was scheduled for my claim. "Yay!" I was advised by the analyst scheduler to expect to hear from the Disability Evaluation Analyst (DEA) soon.

ANOTHER HELPFUL TIP: if you have the opportunity to speak with a DEA scheduler and they know who will be selected as your DEA, always remember <u>before</u> hanging up the telephone "to ask" for your DEA's name and contact information, such as their telephone number. This will help ensure you will be able to speak/connect with your DEA sooner versus later. Remember, those 3P's always be "Prepared, Professional and Polite." **SF#1: System Work Flow and SF#2: People Interaction/cCI**

Back to real time. In a few days, I received an envelope from my DEA via Postal mail with enclosed documents dated, February 6, 2013. "Wow." Well, February 2013 came with much sunshine of activity and hope, with requested documentation and medical exam(s). February and March were very active months and many **"Secret Factors"** were activated. **Quick question: what if I had never called on February 5th to activate the Secret Factors? Answer:** Found out from a SSA source that normal processing takes approximately 2-3 weeks for a DEA to be scheduled. **Secret Factors in Action!** Let's keep moving.

As mentioned, in February medical request forms were sent to me via Postal mail pertaining to verification of my type of illness and disability. I reviewed the package and noticed the following: cover page, fill-in forms, and a return envelope. "Excellent!" It's now time to activate **SF1 and SF2!** The forms displayed my Disability Evaluation Analyst's (DEA's) name and my Case Number (a new number). Unfortunately, there was no contact number information for the DEA, so, it's time for **SF2!** I recommend that you contact your local Social Security Administration office contact person and ask them for your DEA contact information. That is what I did – and it worked! SF#2: People Interaction/cCI

When you secure your DEA telephone number, then call that person and introduce yourself and ask them if they can help you expedite your medical forms, additional reports and -- **what you can do to help them make it easier to process your application**. And, always remember to ask for their direct telephone number and fax number. The DEA position is very busy and therefore, do not expect to have lengthy conversations with them. Therefore, when communicating with your DEA, be prepared to ask a quick question and also expect a "quick" answer.

[RULE #5: Always be respectful of your Social Security Administration contacts. They are extremely busy and do not have time for long discussions or additional stress.] When your process is completed, I recommend you write them a letter or note of thanks for their hard work efforts and in helping you.

The medical exams requested were pertinent to my disability. I had to engage in two (2) medical examinations. The exam process was very structured and customer focused. The exam cost is covered by the SSA. The exams are for evaluation only, and not for treatment. Post cards and reminders with a map were mailed out prior to the exam, along with scheduled date, time and address of examination and a telephone number for questions.

Prior to the medical exams, I had to complete reports requesting information on my illness, such as descriptions, witnesses, daily activities, personal care, meals, ability to get around, social activities, hobbies and interests, coupled with requesting information about my abilities, medications and an open page for **"REMARKS."** **SF#2: People Interaction/cCI** Friendly reminder: when a "REMARKS" section is available on any report – always remember to state your case with the 3P's and double check for accuracy.

The medical examination reports are sent to your home via Postal mail. As mentioned, the reports cover the type of medical appointment, date, time, location and is sent from your DEA. There will also be forms to complete and return back to your DEA via Postal mail with an enclosed return envelope to a PO Box in another city. **SF1 ALERT!!** Whenever a return envelope is enclosed, look on the cover page of the documents to locate a fax number.

The majority of data requested from your DEA will have an enclosed return envelope and a cover sheet that will include a "fax number" option that gives you the opportunity to fax your information. Please note, this fax number is not your DEA's direct fax line. It is a fax number that scans your fax and sends your data to your DEA. Again, this step is very imperative to use, as it **removes approximately one week** of **delayed time** in using Postal mail, versus **<u>faxing</u> within one minute.** Also, it is important to closely follow the instructions on these medical examination forms, and remember to triple check for accuracy.

As mentioned, the SSA works with the Department of Social Services within their Disability Determination Service Division (DDSD) in order to complete the claim for medical development and additional evaluation. There are various forms this division generates to claimants, such as an Adult Report; Adult Report—Third Party, etc. The DEA will send these forms to you and the documents to be completed by a third party (someone who knows you well and is in regular contact with you). These reports are requested to be returned back to your DEA within 10 days via Postal mail. **SF1 ALERT!!**

But, once again there is a fax number located on the cover page and for Work Flow efficiency, I strongly recommend to fax this Third Party form back to your DEA. Also, advise your third party to be consistent and accurate in completing the form and to not leave answers blank. Also, just as important as your report, let your third party reference know the importance to use the "REMARKS" section to explain items that may need clarification to the DEA reader. Remember your third party reference is very essential to help validate your condition and is essential to the process.

Decision Made, Sign-Off, Quality Review

First of all – give KUDOS to yourself, the SSA, your third party reference and to the entire process of SSDI. It is almost done – Yay!

So…let's get back to my sharing of this journey's timeline. The medical exams have been completed, all medical records have been received, and now it is "Decision Making" time. I just had my last SSDI medical exam, all documentation was faxed and the date is March 16, 2013. Whew.

Now was the time to go online and check the status of my application. On March 18, 2013 I went online, and it was stated that a decision was still in the process. I did expect to see that notice, since it was only two (2) days since all of my documentation and last medical exam were completed. Then, March 20th came and I decided to log in and check my status again. I thought maybe in another two days, I would see something to make my day – and I did!!

On March 20, 2013, my status report information read as follows: "A decision has been made on your claim. You will receive the official notice of any decision made on your claim by U.S. mail." Then, the last paragraph showed this: "If you need more information you may call us toll-free at …" SF1 and SF2 ALERT!! Secret factors ready for takeoff and action! I immediately called the toll-free number to find out next steps.

The SSA representative was very kind and we chatted for a couple of minutes and she confirmed a decision had been made on my claim. I did ask the result, and was told the next step would be a Quality Review to ensure all items were verified and confirmed. I was told the Quality Review would take approximately 60 days from that date, and I should receive my decision answer by May 19, 2013. "OH NO!!!"

We cannot have another waiting period, but can we? So, **SF2** went into action and the relationship of asking by using the 3P's was covered: what are the next steps, explain the process, etc. And, we also discussed what could be done to expedite the process. She recommended for me to call back to my local Social Security office in five (5) business days. From that point I said, "Thank you. I will wait five (5) business days, and call my local Social Security office contact person." Basically, I repeated what she said to ensure I was listening.

Wow! So close, but, yet so far. Sixty (60) more days of waiting for the Quality Review. Ugh. But, I had faith, and felt it all would result in my favor. I just felt it, prayed and believed.

The Notice of Award

After waiting five (5) business days, I decided to put SF1 and
SF2 into action and called my local Social Security contact.
Unfortunately, they were not available so I had to leave a
voicemail. But, my voicemail was **SF2** into action. For your
information, here is a summary of the voicemail. As
requested, I gave my name, claim number and then reminded
my local SSA contact who I was, and that we had our first
connection via telephone back in December, and it had been
awhile since we last interacted. Then, I started the reason for
my call with excitement, and used the 3P's to the maximum!

For example, reminding my local SSA contact of our
previous conversations; giving thanks for their support; and
how important they are to me and all the disability claimants
needing their help, etc. My local SSA contact person called
me back within 24 hours and verbally gave me the good
news, that my claim was approved and that I should receive
my Notice of Award in a few days! The Quality Review was
expedited and all was approved!! The local SSA contact
person was happy for me, and I requested them to "please"
fax me a copy of the Notice of Award. Surprisingly, the

Notice of Award was immediately faxed to me on March 28, 2013 at 10:37 a.m. Yay!

Let's quickly review the success of **SF1 and SF2** being combined and activated:

1.) The Quality Review of six (6) weeks was expedited.

2.) Regular work process flow would have taken The Notice of Award to arrive via Postal mail in a few days versus immediate fax. The original was sent via Postal mail, but the fax was immediate verification to confirm The Notice of Award was approved.

3.) With combining **SF#1: System Work Flow and SF#2: People Interaction and/or cCI** by building "real" relationships, it helped expedite the process to have The Notice of Award in my hand immediately, and it brought much peace, hope, and comfort to our home.

Since I **applied for Disability On-My-Own**, the back payments were paid to me in full **(no attorney or advocate fees)**, and monthly disability payments started the following month.

In closing of this process, my personal checklist of completion is as follows:

- Online application completed December 10, 2012.

- The Notice of Award faxed and in hand March 28, 2013. The same faxed document hard copy letter, was dated and mailed via Postal Service on March 31, 2013. **SF1 and SF2** in action to the end-result.

- **Mission Accomplished. Praise the Lord!**

THE BEGINNING OF A "NEW LIFE" CHAPTER

What a journey we had with the writing of this book. I truly hope these words, instructions, and the Secret Factors will help your online process to receive – your hard-earned Social Security Disability Insurance (SSDI) "on-your-own" – is very successful the first time!

The key to starting your "New Life Chapter" is to realize your life has changed. You are now classified as disabled on Social Security Disability Insurance, and unable to work. Some of you will regain strength, be restored health-wise, and in a couple or few years may be able to go back to work, or volunteer to help others in need. That would be wonderful!

Thank God, as of this writing I am still in my "New Life Chapter" of restoration and recovery. After approximately 1½ years of being on Social Security Disability Insurance, I had to return to the operating room and had an equivalent of three (3) surgeries within four (4) weeks on my brain, sinus and skull. Amazing. God is good! I am so thankful for living, and to share these Secret Factors with all of you.

I am not the same young, super-energized J.D. that I was known for being, but, I have a vision/mission, strong faith, perseverance, and a drive to share and help others. I am still in a recovery mode, but, it is important this book comes out immediately in order to help SSDI applicants, who want to **apply on their own** without attorney/advocate assistance. Remember, if you are of sound mind and can manage the following:

1.) Read with understanding.
2.) Use a computer comfortably.
3.) Feel comfortable and confident to speak on your own behalf to an SSA representative and,
4.) Believe you can take control, then **APPLY ON-YOUR-OWN** and reap all of your benefits!

In closing, live life the way you want to live it, and remember to activate the Secret Factors to get what you desire in the essence of life. **Godspeed, and much success to you!**

FIVE "CAN-DO" RULES TO REMEMBER

RULE #1: Contact your local Social Security Administration (SSA) representative immediately, once you receive their contact information to start building your "one-on-one" relationship.

RULE #2: Always find out what FAX number can be used to expedite your application processing.

RULE #3: Take your time to complete your entire application, especially the **Adult Disability Report** section. It is imperative you **ensure accuracy and triple check** your data on all areas of your application.

RULE #4: Keep all receipts and confirmation notices received by SSA close at hand, and do not share your confirmation and re-entry numbers with anyone, unless that person is assisting with your application and needs to process your personal identification data and disability information.

RULE #5: Always be respectful of your Social Security Administration contact(s) time, role, and responsibility. They are extremely busy, and do not have doodle time for long discussions or additional stress. Remember to build your relationships respectfully, and with professionalism and kindness.

THE ROAD MAP To: "YOU CAN DO THIS!"

As noted, this book has two parts – Part One is to assist with help in stabilizing your emotional state, and to focus on being positive and adjusting to a new season of change. Part Two of the book covers "how to" apply for Social Security Disability Insurance with personal examples to assist in understanding the online disability application process.

While writing, I felt it would be helpful to have a solid and easy **"Road Map"** in "how to" do this application process, and named it, **"You Can Do This!"** As mentioned, I did it "on-my-own" and so can you! Remember in the beginning of Part Two, the first chapter "What's the Secret?" covers the secret factors of focus which are: Secret Factor (SF) #1: System Work Flow, Secret Factor (SF) #2: People Interaction/cCI (conduced Customer Intimacy). These Secret Factors are very helpful in navigating through the overall disability application process.

To make it an easier process, following is a road map of the expedited steps, and what to look for while completing your application with reference to the Secret Factors. Please remember to read **ALL** of your **SSDI** application information, and do **NOT** only use this checklist to complete your disability application.

Social Security Disability Insurance application updates and changes are <u>always</u> being conducted via the Internet, therefore as mentioned – <u>DO NOT</u> only use this Road Map checklist to complete your disability application.

Also, it is imperative you do not give a quick glance over the SSDI actual application and information requested, but use this book of information ONLY as *"reference tips"* to assist in ways **to expedite your disability application process.**

The ROAD MAP: "You Can Do This!!"

<u>NOTE</u>: Each SSA Disability Insurance applicant and case is different. The following is an example of what may occur, as it did from personal experience. The following **does not guarantee** the exact process will occur in the same format, but, the **"Secret Factors and 3P's"** are solid recommendations that will significantly assist you with this process – and also with life in general as it relates to dealing with consumer to business relationships. For example: having an issue to resolve with a business colleague, store manager, etc. When you have completed each of the following numbered **"Road Map"** tips, check the square box to the left of the number to ensure completion of that tactic. See following checked example when completed: ☑

☐ 1.) Once you find out that you have a disabling illness, and it is confirmed for a significant period of time, immediately sign-up and register on the **Internet** for your Social Security Disability Insurance (SSDI) benefit claim. Go to the website: www.socialsecurity.gov/applyfordisability

    a. NOTE: as of September 2014, the SSDI online application website is available for applying the following days and hours (Eastern Time): Monday-Friday: 5 a.m. – 1 a.m.; Saturday: 5 a.m. – 11 p.m.; Sunday: 8 a.m. – 10 p.m. *(days and times may change)*

☐ 2.) Review the Social Security Starter Disability Kit to ensure you qualify to apply online. If so, move forward! **SF#1: System Work Flow**

☐ 3.) Complete first section of SSDI application process, which is called the, "Disability Benefit Application."
SF#1: System Work Flow

☐ 4.) Once completed, you will receive confirmation of the Disability Benefit Application being completed via an online notification. SF#1: System Work Flow

☐ 5.) Next, you will receive a hard copy letter in the mail stating next steps such as, if additional information is requested for verification of proof of income, etc.; and to complete the second section of the online SSDI application process which is called the, **Adult Disability Report.** SF#1: System Work Flow

☐ 6.) If SSA does request additional documents, such as verifying proof of income, etc. contact your SSA representative via telephone, and request they give you their fax number to expedite sending proof of income versus sending it through U.S. Postal Service (USPS) mail.

SF#1: System Work Flow and SF#2: People Interaction/cCI

☐ 7.) The Adult Disability Report (ADR) is a separate report and covers details of explaining your illness, medication, doctors, etc. and is a very important document that "states your case." The ADR has its own **"Re-entry Number"** for access back and forth into the Internet application system. Read the ADR closely, follow the details, and triple check your work. Most important, do not share your Re-Entry Number with anyone, and ensure you use the designated Sign-Off-"Finish later option." SSDI will save your last completed data entered, and when you're fresh and ready to proceed with your application again, re-enter back into the system and it will display your last entry. SF#1: System Work Flow

☐ 8.) The ADR has a "REMARKS" section at the end of the application. It is imperative you use this section to tell your story, express your passion and request your need.

SF#1: System Work Flow and SF#2: People Interaction/cCI

☐ 9.) The online Medical Release form will need to be completed at this time. Recommend to continue online and use e-signature to approve the form, if you concur. Then, you are done. | SF#1: System Work Flow |

☐ 10.) Once you have completed your ADR and electronically signed and dated your Medical Release Form you will receive a confirmation! | SF#1: System Work Flow |

☐ 11.) You should receive a form letter from your local SSA office acknowledging receipt of your application, and informing you how to check the Status of your Claim. | SF#1: System Work Flow |

☐ 12.) There is a waiting period where medical information has been requested from your doctors, hospitals, etc. and being reviewed. Also, your claim will now be moved and worked in another department and division to schedule medical examinations, etc. Additionally, a new team will handle your claim, for evaluation called, Disability Evaluation Analysts

(DEA). This team is under the Department of Social Services, and is in the Division of Disability Determinations (DDS).

SF1 and SF2 MAXIMIZED!

☐ 13.) Many Secret Factors occur during the above #12's System Flow and People Interaction/cCI process, and it is highly recommended to closely read the section, "Medical Examinations and Other Documentations" to completely understand how to manage through the process expeditiously without an issue. **SF1 and SF2 ALERT!!**

☐ 14.) A Decision will be made, and there will be a Sign-Off and Quality Review process. The timing varies in each of these areas and the key will be to stay focused on patience, system work flow, cCI, people interaction and diligent follow-up using the 3P's. **SF#2: People Interaction/cCI**

☐ 15.) If all of the aforementioned is completed with **favor** of your claim, you will receive **"The Notice of Award"** for your Social Security Disability Insurance claim.

Congratulations!!!

**You successfully did it, and
Applied for Disability "On-Your-Own!"**

REFERENCES AND RESOURCES

CBS 60 Minutes Overtime. *"Disability, USA"* aired October 6, 2013, Rebroadcast on June 29, 2014. www.cbsnews.com/news/disability-usa-2

Friday, Tony. (Posted July 17, 2011 12:47PM) Working in Silos. *Leadership Perspectives Causing Excellence.* http://leadershipperspectives.blogspot.com/2011/07/working-in-silos.html

Lowe, Greg. (Posted June 4, 2012) Breaking down silos, that does that mean? *@Greg2dot0'sBlog.* http://greg2dot0.com/2012/06/04/breaking-down-silos/

The American Heritage Dictionary of the English Language, Fourth Edition. (2000) Boston, MA: Houghton Mifflin Company.

The Holy Bible, New King James Version. (1988) Nashville, TN: Thomas Nelson Publishers.

U.S. Social Security Administration. Web. http://www.socialsecurity.gov November 17, 2012 to November 19, 2014.

U.S. Social Security Administration. Web.
http://www.socialsecurity.gov/applyfordisability
November 17, 2012 to November 19, 2014.

www.ingramcontent.com/pod-product-compliance
Lightning Source LLC
LaVergne TN
LVHW021526080426
835509LV00018B/2679

9 780986 387609